G. B. Trudeau's *Doonesbury* is featured in over 500 daily newspapers including the *Guardian*. It is still the only comic strip to have been awarded the Pulitzer Prize (1975) and, in addition, G. B. Trudeau has received thirteen honorary degrees.

**Also by G. B. Trudeau in Abacus:**

*THAT'S* DOCTOR *SINATRA, YOU LITTLE BIMBO*
*READ MY LIPS,  MAKE MY DAY,  EAT QUICHE AND DIE*

# A DOONESBURY BOOK
## by G. B. TRUDEAU

# GIVE THOSE NYMPHS SOME HOOTERS!

ABACUS

An Abacus Book

First published in Great Britain in Abacus by
Sphere Books Ltd 1990

Copyright © G. B. Trudeau 1989

*All characters in this publication are fictitious
and any resemblance to real persons, living or dead,
is purely coincidental.*

ISBN 0349 0188 4

Printed and bound in Great Britain by
BPCC Hazell Books
Aylesbury, Bucks, England
Member of BPCC Ltd.

A Division of
Macdonald & Co (Publishers) Ltd
Orbit House
1 New Fetter Lane
London EC4A 1AR
A member of Maxwell Macmillan Pergamon Publishing Corporation

"Donald starts out each day talking to the doormen at the Trump Tower. The doormen love him. He is a man of the people."

— From Donald Trump's résumé

ZOOM! ZOOM!

ANYTHING ELSE, SIR?

YEAH. I WANT A BIG PARTY TO ANNOUNCE MY NEW AIR-LINE SHUTTLE SERVICE!

YES, SIR. HAVE YOU DECIDED YET WHAT YOU'RE GOING TO CALL IT?

WHAT DO YOU THINK? I'M NAMING IT AFTER MY-SELF! MY NAME MEANS QUALITY! IT'S **SYNONYMOUS** WITH QUAL-ITY!

"DONALD" IS SYNON-YMOUS WITH QUALITY, SIR?

NO, DUMMY— "TRUMP"! AS IN TRUMP PLAZA! TRUMP PRINCESS! TRUMP CITY! IVANA TRUMP!

OH...

STILL, YOU RAISE A GOOD POINT. CALL MY LAWYERS AND TELL THEM I WANT TO LEGALLY RENAME MYSELF!

AFTER YOURSELF, SIR?

TRUMP T. TRUMP! I LIKE IT! IT **SCREAMS** QUALITY!

WE'RE PROJECTING AN 89 DEFICIT OF OVER $5 MILLION? STAN, HOW IS THIS POSSIBLE?

IT'S BECAUSE OUR TUITION INCOME IS OFF, SIR.

OUR FRESHMAN CLASS IS THE SMALLEST IT'S BEEN IN YEARS. AND WE CAN'T FILL IT UP WITHOUT LOWERING OUR ADMISSION STANDARDS EVEN FURTHER THAN WE ALREADY HAVE!

OH.

HOW LOW IS THAT?

WELL, CURRENTLY WE DON'T ACCEPT ANYONE WITH A CRIMINAL RECORD.

WHAT I'M SUGGESTING, MR. PRESIDENT, IS THAT WALDEN COLLEGE NEEDS OUTSIDE HELP...

OUTSIDE HELP? FOR WHAT?

FOR RECRUITING STUDENTS! WE NEED AN AGGRESSIVE MARKETING PROGRAM!

ONE OF OUR RECENT GRADS IS NOW WORKING FOR A MAJOR AD AGENCY. I THINK WE SHOULD CONTACT HIM. THE WORD IS HE DOES VERY CLASSY WORK!

GOOD, SHARON, GOOD! NOW RUB YOUR LEG UP AGAINST THE PRODUCT!

OW! DAMN!

YOU'RE NEVER GOING TO BELIEVE WHAT ACCOUNT I LANDED TODAY! WALDEN COLLEGE! THEY WANT ME TO HELP THEM WITH RECRUITMENT SPOTS!

APPARENTLY, WALDEN'S GOT SOMETHING OF A FUZZY IMAGE IN THE MARKET...

WALDEN COLLEGE... WHY DOES THAT RING A BELL?...

BECAUSE YOU WENT THERE! YOU'RE A GRADUATE!

OH, SURE, RIGHT, I KNEW THAT.

SEE, THIS IS EXACTLY THE PROBLEM...

WAIT, ARE YOU SURE? I THOUGHT I WENT TO TRADE SCHOOL...

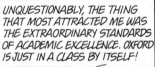

WHEN FIRST I SAW CATALOGUE, I ASK, "WHAT IS THIS WALDEN?"

I LEARN IT HAS CAMPUS TO WHICH COME STUDENTS FROM MANY CITIES, MANY STATES...

I CRY TO LEARN SUCH THINGS. IT SEEMS TO ME THAT WALDEN IS SHINING CITY ON HILL, SO BEAUTIFUL IS THIS COL-LEGE.

WHAT'S WITH THE POLISH DIALECT?

SHE'S GOING THROUGH A STREEP THING. LET ME TALK WITH HER.

WHICH WAY DO I LOOK?

DIRECTLY INTO THE CAMERA. WE'RE READY WHEN YOU ARE.

UH...OKAY, HERE'S THE DEAL. I WENT TO WALDEN BECAUSE, YOU KNOW, I'D HEARD REALLY GOOD STUFF ABOUT IT...

WHAT KIND OF STUFF?

WELL, STUFF LIKE THE PLACE WAS AWESOME, STUFF LIKE THAT. SO ANYWAY...

CUT! THAT'S A WRAP!

WAIT A MINUTE, I HAVEN'T EVEN SAID...

IT'S PERFECT! WE'RE SHOWING THAT ATHLETES ARE WEL-COME, TOO.

THE STILLS CAME OUT GREAT, DON'T YOU THINK, BOOPSIE?

BOY... NOW I'VE SEEN EVERY-THING!

WHAT'S THAT?

THERE'S A WOMAN ON CHANNEL Z GIVING BIRTH LIVE ON THE AIR!

YOU'RE KIDDING. OH, MY GOD...

YOU KNOW, SHE LOOKS VERY FAMILIAR. SHE LOOKS LIKE... LIKE...

J.J.!

NO...NO, MORE LIKE SALLY FIELD.

10

11

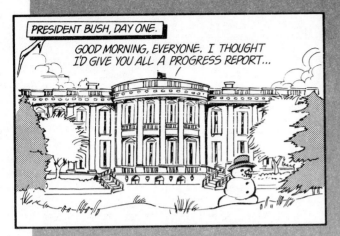

15

A WINTRY EVE AT THE CEMETERY IN KINDERHOOK, NEW YORK.

HEY, JOSH! OVER HERE!

MARTIN van BUREN

1782-1862

LOVING FATHER PRESIDENT

WHAT IS IT, HENRY?

LOOK! SOMEONE'S DUG UP MARTIN VAN BUREN'S COFFIN!

MY GOD! THEY'VE... TAKEN HIS...HIS SKULL!

I CAN'T BELIEVE IT! WHO WOULD COMMIT SUCH A GHOULISH AND DASTARDLY CRIME?

WHO, INDEED.

WE'LL NOW HAVE A REPORT FROM THE ACQUISITIONS COMMITTEE!

GOOD NEWS, LADS!

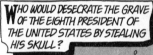

WHO WOULD DESECRATE THE GRAVE OF THE EIGHTH PRESIDENT OF THE UNITED STATES BY STEALING HIS SKULL?

THE ANSWER LAY BEHIND THE MENACING FACADE OF THE YALE SECRET SOCIETY KNOWN AS SKULL AND BONES...

...WHERE TO COMMEMORATE THE PRESIDENTIAL VICTORY OF ITS MOST DISTINGUISHED MEMBER...

...A TROPHY WAS BEING INSTALLED.

PUT HIM BETWEEN GERONIMO AND ELVIS!

THE MOOD AT THE SKULL AND BONES TRUSTEES MEETING WAS EXULTANT.

MAY I JUST COMMEND THE ACQUISITIONS COMMITTEE FOR A JOB WELL DONE?

HEAR! HEAR!

THE SKULL OF MARTIN VAN BUREN, THE LAST SITTING VICE PRESIDENT TO BE ELECTED PRESIDENT, MAKES A FITTING TRIBUTE TO THE RECENT TRIUMPH OF OUR OWN POPPY BUSH!

IN TIMELINESS AND DEGREE OF DIFFICULTY, THE PINCHING OF VAN BUREN'S SKULL HAS TO BE CONSIDERED THE MOST REMARKABLE ACQUISITION BY A MEMBER IN YEARS!

AHEM!

OH. WITH THE POSSIBLE EXCEPTION OF TODD'S HEIST OF ISADORA DUNCAN'S THIGH BONE.

THANK YOU.

THE SOCIETY'S DISPLAY CASES, WHILE OVERCROWDED, ARE WIDELY CONCEDED TO HOLD THE WORLD'S FINEST PRIVATE COLLECTION OF SKULLS...

...INCLUDING THOSE OF SOME OF HISTORY'S MOST ILLUSTRIOUS FIGURES, SUCH AS KIERKEGAARD, MADAME CURIE, NAPOLEON...

N. BONAPA

...AND THE SOCIETY'S MOST PRIZED CATCH—**TUTANKHAMEN,** PINCHED BY A BOARD MEMBER OF THE METROPOLITAN MUSEUM OF ART.

TUTANKHAMEN

LESS WELL-KNOWN IS THE SOCIETY'S GAG COLLECTION...

HI! I'M DR. LIVINGSTONE!

HA, HA, HA!

**STOP** IT! YOU'RE **KILLING** US!

AN UNSUSPECTING PRESIDENT-ELECT ARRIVES FOR THE WINTER MEETING OF SKULL AND BONES.

POPPY, WE'VE GOT A LITTLE SURPRISE FOR YOU!

YOU DO?

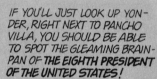

IF YOU'LL JUST LOOK UP YONDER, RIGHT NEXT TO PANCHO VILLA, YOU SHOULD BE ABLE TO SPOT THE GLEAMING BRAINPAN OF **THE EIGHTH PRESIDENT OF THE UNITED STATES!**

WHAT?

YOU MEAN, YOU FELLOWS PINCHED THE SKULL OF MARTIN VAN BUREN JUST TO HONOR **ME?** I DON'T **BELIEVE** IT! THAT'S JUST **SO** THOUGHTFUL!

WELL, WE JUST FELT... WHAT ARE YOU DOING?

WRITING YOU GUYS A THANK-YOU NOTE!

THE PRESENTATION.

POPPY, IN YOUR HONOUR, WE HAVE ACQUIRED THE SKULL OF **MARTIN VAN BUREN!**

BESIDES BEING THE LAST SITTING VICE PRESIDENT TO BECOME PRESIDENT, VAN BUREN, LIKE YOU, WAS A MAN OF TREMENDOUS ACCOMPLISHMENTS, SUCH AS...

SUCH AS... UM...

WELL, ANYWAY, WE THOUGHT IT WAS REALLY APPROPRIATE.

IT **IS!** IT'S A NEAT CONNECTION, YOU GUYS!

THE TRUTH IS, TAD HAD NEVER REALLY FIT INTO THE BROTHERHOOD. HE WAS A "BONESMAN" IN NAME ONLY.

WHEN HE COULD NO LONGER STILL THE VOICE OF CONSCIENCE, HE PLACED A DESPERATE CALL.

ASSOCIATED PRESS? LISTEN CAREFULLY. THE PURLOINED SKULL OF MARTIN VAN BUREN IS IN THE SKULL AND BONES MAUSOLEUM!

HEY, THANKS FOR THE TIP. WHAT'S YOUR NAME, BUDDY? ...BUDDY?

OF COURSE, FROM THAT MOMENT ON, HE WAS DAMNED FOR ETERNITY.

MY GOD... WHAT HAVE I DONE?

WHEN THE PRESS HORDES ARRIVED, ONLY SPECIAL AGENTS TURNER AND MADISON WERE ON DUTY.

WHAT THE...?

WITHIN HOURS, THE SITUATION OUTSIDE THE BONES MAUSOLEUM WAS NEARLY OUT OF CONTROL.

BRONCO, INFORM MOONWALKER WE'VE GOT A CROWD OF ABOUT 300 OUT HERE!

WE'VE ALSO GOT A NEW HAVEN D.A. HERE WITH A SEARCH WARRANT! SOMETHING ABOUT—GET THIS—STOLEN SKULLS!

NO GO, LADS! THEY'RE TOO BIG!

FOOSH! FOOSH!

WHAT ABOUT PANCHO VILLA?

NO PROBLEM. HE WAS A GIFT FROM MEXICO.

AS WORD OF THE LURID ALLEGATIONS SPREAD, THE CROWD OUTSIDE THE TOMB BEGAN TO SWELL.

AND SINCE THE STENCH OF DEATH WILL ALWAYS ATTRACT FLIES AND VERMIN...

DISPERSE AT ONCE!

PO

...THE ARRIVAL OF GERALDO WAS PERHAPS INEVITABLE.

PLEASE! I BEG YOU! DO NOT LET YOUR CHILDREN WATCH THIS!

B-B-B BRAT!

MEANWHILE, INSIDE, THE TRAITOR HAD BEEN FOUND.

YOU'RE IN DEEP DOO-DOO, FELLAH!

NOOO!

23

24

YOU KNOW WHAT THEY SAY ABOUT US BABY SITTERS, DON'T YOU, BABY DOE?

> GURGLE! <
GLUP!

THEY SAY WE CHARGE EXORBITANT FEES FOR SITTING AROUND WATCHING SILLY GAME SHOWS AND SCARFING DOWN OTHER PEOPLE'S FOOD!

SQUEAK! SQUEAK!

THAT'S THE POPULAR IMAGE, ANYWAY. WELL, YOU WANT TO KNOW WHAT MY PHILOSOPHY ABOUT THAT IS?

SQUEAK!

WHY FIGHT IT?

OKAY! LET'S SEE WHAT VANNA'S WEARING TODAY!

CLIK!

GB Trudeau

I CAN'T BELIEVE WE JUST LEFT LITTLE NO-NAME WITH ZONKER.

SHE'LL BE FINE.

WHAT IF HE JUST PLOPS HER IN FRONT OF THE TUBE AND ZONES OUT ALL DAY?

HE WON'T. HE TOLD ME HIMSELF HE DOESN'T BELIEVE IN UNSUPERVISED TELEVISION.

GB Trudeau

OKAY, NOW, THAT'S CALLED "CROSS-DRESSING." CAN YOU SAY "CROSS-DRESSING"?

TRY THE PEARLS, PHIL!

WELL, THAT'S IT, BABY DOE! YOU CAN CARRY ON ALL YOU WANT, BUT NO MORE TUBE FOR TODAY!

CLIK!

THERE'S MORE TO LIFE THAN GERALDO AND OPRAH AND SALLY AND PHIL AND MORTON AND GARY AND REGIS AND PEE-WEE!

INCREDIBLE AS IT SOUNDS, THERE'S A WHOLE WORLD OUTSIDE OF TELEVISION, BABY DOE! THERE'S CENTRAL PARK, THE MUSEUM OF NATURAL HISTORY, THE BRONX ZOO!

WHAT? YOU SAY YOU WANT TO WATCH "A CURRENT AFFAIR"? WELL, OKAY, BUT THAT'S IT!

NEXT, SHE FEDERAL EXPRESSED HER HUSBAND'S HEAD TO HIS LOVER...

CLIK!

GB Trudeau

SO HOW'S MEXICO, BOOPSIE?

FABULOUS, B.D.!

WE HAVEN'T STARTED SHOOTING YET, BUT SO FAR, THE "SPORTS ILLUSTRATED" PEOPLE HAVE TREATED ME **VERY** WELL.

THEY BETTER.

HONESTLY, I DON'T SEE WHY THE SWIMSUIT ISSUE IS SO CONTROVERSIAL. I THINK IT'S NICE THAT ONCE A YEAR THERE'S AN ISSUE OF THE MAGAZINE JUST FOR WOMEN READERS!

UH... WOMEN READERS?

TO HELP THEM CHOOSE BEACH APPAREL! WHY DO YOU THINK IT'S SUCH A BIG SELLER?

OKAY, HERE'S ALL THE STUFF YOU'LL NEED, HONEY. BE SURE TO USE LOTS OF THE SUN BLOCK.

OKAY.

USE THE HAIR STREAK TONIGHT. THERE WON'T BE TIME TO SUN BLEACH IT BEFORE THE SHOOT.

YES, MA'AM.

LET'S HAVE YOU TRY ON THE SWIMSUIT NOW, OKAY?

OKAY. WHERE IS IT?

UH... I JUST GAVE IT TO YOU.

THIS? OH, SORRY, I THOUGHT IT WAS DENTAL FLOSS.

OKAY, BOOPSIE, IF YOU'LL JUST DROP THE ROBE, WELL BOOGIE!

WELL... OKAY...

SOMETHING WRONG, KID?

WELL, YES, IN A WAY. I GUESS I DON'T FEEL COMFORTABLE YET. I FEEL LIKE I'M POSING FOR "PENTHOUSE".

HONEY, I CAN ASSURE YOU, THERE'S A **WORLD** OF DIFFERENCE BETWEEN "PENTHOUSE" AND "SPORTS ILLUSTRATED"! JUST RELAX AND... GOOD... VERY GOOD... WHY, BOOPSIE, YOU'RE A NATURAL! GOOD!

CLIK! CLIK! CLIK! CLIK! CLIK!

OKAY, GREAT! NOW, LET'S TRY A FEW WITH THE SUIT ON!

IT **WAS** ON! SEE, THAT'S WHAT I MEAN!

32

33

...AND A NATIONAL SURVEY, COMMISSIONED ESPECIALLY FOR THE TOBACCO INDUSTRY, FOUND THAT A MAJORITY OF AMERICANS DO **NOT** SUPPORT MORE RESTRICTIVE ANTI-SMOKING MEASURES!

YOU'VE BEEN LISTENING TO THE BASSO PROFUNDO OF DEAR OLD DAD, RECENTLY ANOINTED COMMUNICATIONS DIRECTOR FOR THE R.J. REYNOLDS COMPANY!

YOU KNOW, DAD, THIS POLL CONTRADICTS EVERY OTHER SURVEY IN RECENT YEARS. MIND IF I TAKE A LOOK?

BE MY GUEST!

"DO YOU FAVOR GESTAPO-STYLE POLICE TACTICS TO PREVENT SMOKING IN PUBLIC?"

OH, SURE, WE COULD QUIBBLE OVER WORDING...

..." AND THE CONTROVERSIAL FINDINGS ABOUT TOBACCO USE SHOULD NOT BE USED TO DEPRIVE SMOKERS OF THEIR RIGHTS AS CITIZENS!"

THANKS, DAD!

FOR LISTENERS WHO DON'T KNOW, I SHOULD EXPLAIN THAT THE WORD "CONTROVERSIAL" IS A TOBACCO INDUSTRY CODE WORD FOR ANY WIDELY ACCEPTED VIEW THAT IS NOT IN THE INDUSTRY'S BEST INTERESTS!

FOR INSTANCE, THE FACT THAT NICOTINE IS AS ADDICTIVE AS HEROIN IS "CONTROVERSIAL," RIGHT, DAD?

OF COURSE. AS IS THE CLAIM THAT PASSIVE SMOKING IS HARMFUL!

AND THE 390,000 DEATHS A YEAR?

ALL OF THEM CONTROVERSIAL! **DEEPLY** DISPUTED!

THE FACT IS, MARK, WHEN YOU TAKE A CLOSE LOOK AT THESE FIGURES, THEY JUST DON'T HOLD UP AS SCARE STATISTICS!

FOR INSTANCE, THE BILLIONS IN "LOST" PRODUCTIVITY! HOW DO WE KNOW THAT ALL THE SMOKERS WHO GOT SICK WOULDN'T HAVE GOTTEN SICK ANYWAY?

LOOK AT ME. AFTER 30 YEARS OF SMOKING, I HAVEN'T MISSED A **SINGLE** DAY OF WORK OWING TO SMOKING-RELATED ILLNESS!

DAD, YOU HAD A HEART ATTACK!

OKAY, SO I MISSED A WEEK. TEN DAYS, TOPS!

36

WELCOME BACK. WE'RE HERE TALKING TO EDITORIAL CARTOONIST HARVEY FOOTE ABOUT THE "CARTOONISTS' HONEYMOON WEEK"!

SO, WHAT'S IT ALL ABOUT, HARV?

WELL, MARK, FOR THE NEXT SEVEN DAYS MY COLLEAGUES AND I HAVE PLEDGED NOT TO RIDICULE THE PRESIDENT!

A LOT OF US HAVE BEEN FEELING A LITTLE LEFT OUT OF THE CURRENT MEDIA HONEYMOON, SO IN THE SPIRIT OF ST. VALENTINE, WE'VE DECIDED TO COMMIT OURSELVES TO A WEEK-LONG BUSH-OUT!

IT'S ALSO OUR WAY OF FORMALLY THANKING BUSH FOR DAN QUAYLE.

LONG OVERDUE, IF YOU ASK ME.

WE, THE UNDERSIGNED, IN ORDER TO HELP GEORGE BUSH GET A HANDLE ON THE VISION THING, DO DECLARE A "CARTOONISTS' HONEYMOON WEEK," AND PLEDGE TO ABSTAIN FROM RIDICULING THE PRESIDENT FOR NO LESS THAN SEVEN DAYS.

OLIPHANT  MIKE PETERS  WASHI
SZEP  AUTH  MCNELLY
MARLETTE  CONRAD
GB Trudeau

... AND A LOT OF OTHER GUYS.

WOW... ALL OF YOU ARE REALLY GOING TO LAY OFF BUSH FOR A **WHOLE WEEK**?

IT'S KIND OF AN EXPERIMENT, MARK. OUR HOPE IS THAT IF WE REMOVE THE FEAR OF RIDICULE, PERHAPS BUSH WILL DO SOMETHING THAT'S ACTUALLY STATESMANLIKE!

WHAT IF HE DOES SOMETHING REALLY, REALLY BUSH-LIKE?

WELL, THAT, OF COURSE, WOULD VIOLATE THE SPIRIT OF THE HONEYMOON. WE'D HAVE TO CALL IT OFF.

WHAT WE CARTOONISTS ARE HOPING TO ENCOURAGE HERE, MARK, ARE SOME BOLD INITIATIVES FROM THE BUSH ADMINISTRATION!

WHAT A LOT OF PEOPLE DON'T UNDERSTAND IS THAT CARTOONISTS ARE PATRIOTS! WE **WANT** TO SEE OUR PRESIDENTS SUCCEED! IF A CARTOONING MORATORIUM HELPS BUSH GET A LITTLE CONFIDENCE, THEN WE'RE HAPPY TO OBLIGE!

SO WE PUT A CAP ON THE VITRIOL FOR A WEEK. WHAT CAN IT HURT? OUR EDITORS ARE PATRIOTIC, TOO. THEY'LL UNDERSTAND.

WILL YOU STILL GET PAID?

OH, SURE. WE'RE ALL TAKING SICK LEAVE.

LET ME SAY THIS ABOUT BUSH, MARK. BY ALL ACCOUNTS, HE'S A NICE, DECENT MAN. HIS STRONG EMPHASIS ON ETHICS IS AS COMMEND-ABLE AS IT IS IN CHARACTER.

HE VIEWS PUBLIC SERVICE AS A PRIVILEGE AND A SACRED TRUST. ANYONE WHO VIOLATES THAT TRUST WILL HAVE NO PLACE IN HIS ADMINISTRATION.

WELL, THAT WAS UPLIFTING. ANY BOLD INITIATIVES YET?

NOTHING ON THE WIRES.

ANOTHER THING ABOUT GEORGE BUSH, MARK. HE DOESN'T JUST **TALK** ABOUT FAMILY VALUES, HE **LIVES** THEM!

HE AND HIS WIFE HAVE BEEN LOVING, CARING PARENTS, AND THE RESULTS SHOW! THIS WHITE HOUSE WILL BE A HAPPY PLACE, RINGING AS IT WILL WITH THE LAUGHTER OF TRULY CHERISHED CHILDREN.

=RING!=

IT WILL SERVE AS AN INSPIRA-TION TO US ALL!

I THINK WE HAVE A CALLER, HARVEY.

IT'S THE BUSHES. THEY WANT A COPY OF THIS FOR THEIR FRIDGE.

THEY COULD JUST CLIP IT, RIGHT?

RIGHT. TELL THEM TO USE THE DOTTED LINES.

ALSO, DID I MENTION HIS MANNERS? GEORGE BUSH IS NOTHING IF NOT POLITE! WHO AMONG US HAS NOT RECEIVED A NOTE FROM HIM AT ONE TIME OR...

UH... HARV?

WHAT?

HARV, IT'S MONDAY.

MONDAY? YOU MEAN...

UH-HUH.

THE HONEY-MOON IS **OVER!**

I THOUGHT WE'D START RIGHT IN ON ETHICS.

THIS JUST IN, CAMPERS! THE FIRST "HIT PARADE OF SHAME" FROM THE BUSH ADMINISTRATION! I KNOW, I KNOW, IT SEEMS A TAD EARLY, BUT WHAT ARE YOU GO-ING TO DO?

LET'S GET TO IT! SENATOR JOHN TOWER, ALLEGATIONS OF DRINK-ING AND WENCHING; REP. JACK KEMP, FINANCIAL IMPROPRIETIES; C. BOYDEN GRAY, ETHICS CHIEF; SAME...

ETHICS CHIEF?

THAT CAN'T BE RIGHT...

SEE WHAT HAPPENS WHEN WE GO OFF THE JOB FOR A WEEK?

LESS THAN ONE MONTH AGO, GEORGE BUSH'S THEME-OF-THE-WEEK WAS ETHICS! HE WOULD NOT TOLERATE, HE TOLD US, EVEN THE **APPEAR-ANCE** OF IMPROPRIETY IN HIS AD-MINISTRATION!

SINCE THEN, WE'VE SEEN JOHN TOW-ER SCANDALIZED BY HIS PECCADIL-LOS INVOLVING WINE, WOMEN AND, ONE ASSUMES, SONG; JACK KEMP, AC-CUSED OF FINAN-CIAL IMPROPRI-ETIES; DITTO, ETHICS CHIEF C. BOYDEN GRAY...

ALL OF THIS DURING THE FIRST TWO WEEKS OF GEORGE BUSH'S WATCH! IS THIS WHAT BUSH MEANT BY... BY...

ACTUALLY, I FEEL KINDA SORRY FOR THE GUY.

DELAYED HONEYMOON SYNDROME.

...AND THE CLUSTER OF PROBLEMS SURROUNDING JOHN TOWER—THE SEEMINGLY ENDLESS STREAM OF ALLEGATIONS—NOW MAKES IT ALMOST UNTHINKABLE THAT THE SENATE WILL VOTE TO CONFIRM HIM AS SECRETARY OF DEFENSE!

WHAT IF IT DOES?

WHAT IF IT DOES, YOU ASK? WELL, BEFORE WE KNOW IT, WE COULD BE LOOKING AT SAM NUNN'S WORST NIGHTMARE!

SAM NUNN'S WORST NIGHTMARE.

JOE'S PIZZA! HA, HA! OH, HI, GENERAL! JES' KIDDIN'! HA, HA! WHAZZUP?

42

BOTTOM LINE, CAMPERS...

WHAT DOES IT SAY ABOUT GEORGE BUSH THAT HE PICKS A SECRETARY OF DEFENSE WITH A HISTORY OF ALCOHOL ABUSE...

... THAT HE PICKS AN ETHICS CHIEF WHO FAILS TO REPORT INCOME, AND A SECRETARY OF HEALTH AND HUMAN SERVICES WHO TRIES TO DOUBLE DIP?

IT SAYS DAN QUAYLE WASN'T A FLUKE!

YOU PEEKED!

WELL, THAT'S IT, HARVEY! THANKS FOR JOINING US!

MY PLEASURE, MARK.

YOU KNOW, HARV, YOU GUYS DID YOURSELF PROUD WITH THIS CARTOONISTS' HONEYMOON. IT WAS A REAL PUBLIC SERVICE!

WOULD YOU EVER CONSIDER EXTENDING IT, YOU KNOW, GETTING BEHIND THE PRESIDENT AND REALLY GIVING THE GUY THE CHANCE?

I'VE GOT A FAMILY, MARK.

ME, NEITHER.

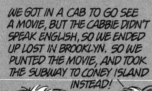

PETER, NOT ALL THE AUTHORS PANNED HERE TODAY RECEIVED DEATH THREATS. LESSER SENTENCES RANGED FROM THE REMOVAL OF A HAND TO A SLAP ON THE WRIST.

AMONG THE NOTABLES, JEFFREY ARCHER HAS BEEN CONDEMNED TO LOSE AN EAR, ERICH SEGAL IS SENTENCED TO A BEATING, AND JACKIE COLLINS WILL RECEIVE 50 LASHES OF THE WHIP.

RESPONSES HAVE VARIED. BOTH SEGAL AND ARCHER HAVE REPORTEDLY HIRED BODYGUARDS AND GONE INTO HIDING...

MS. COLLINS, ON THE OTHER HAND, IS SAID TO BE LOOKING FORWARD TO HER SENTENCE.

... AND LAST NIGHT'S EVENTS ARE UTTERLY REPUGNANT TO ALL WHO VALUE FREEDOM OF EXPRESSION!

WHILE NONE OF US IS ABOVE CONSTRUCTIVE CRITICISM, THE TEHERAN PANS ARE A GROSS AFFRONT TO THIS LIT'RY LIFE AS WE KNOW IT!

ACCORDINGLY, WE, THE MEMBERS OF THE AUTHORS GUILD, DO HEREBY **CONDEMN** THE BARBAROUS THREATS ON THE LIVES OF OUR COLLEAGUES MICHAEL KORDA, SIDNEY SHELDON AND LEO BUSCAGLIA!

HOWEVER, IN THE SPIRIT OF COMPROMISE, WE RELUCTANTLY SUPPORT THE STONING OF DONALD TRUMP.

CLAP! CLAP! CLAP! CLAP!

GUESS WHAT? THE GALLERY CALLED. I GOT ANOTHER BATHROOM GIG!

WHAT?

IT'S A COMMISSION FOR A THREE-ROOM SERIES OF WALL AND CEILING MURALS!

THAT'S GREAT! WHO'S THE CLIENT?

I DUNNO, SOME RICH GUY. BUT GET THIS—THE BATHROOMS ARE ON HIS BOAT!

HIS BOAT?

New York Times

...AND UP THERE OVER THE JOHN, I WANT A BIG BUNCH OF NYMPHS!

I'LL TELL HER, MR. TRUMP.

WELCOME ABOARD THE "TRUMP PRINCESS," J.J.! MR. TRUMP IS LOOKING FORWARD TO MEETING YOU!

THANKS, HONEY...

THESE ARE THE ARCHITECT'S DRAWINGS FOR THE BATHROOMS. MR. TRUMP HAS INDICATED WHERE HE WANTS THE MURALS...

OKAY.

HE'S LOOKING FOR SCENES OF EPIC GRANDEUR. IN THE MASTER BATH, HE WANTS THE PARTING OF THE RED SEA. IN HIS WIFE'S BOUDOIR, THE CORONATION OF CATHERINE THE GREAT...

WHAT'S THAT SCENE OVER THE TUB?

UM...I BELIEVE THAT'S THE 1981 EVICTION OF HIS RENT CONTROL TENANTS.

DO YOU THINK WE COULD GET ANY OF THEM TO MODEL?

BEFORE I TELL MR. TRUMP YOU'RE HERE, MISS, I BETTER SHOW YOU THE MASTER BATHROOM.

WHY'S THAT?

ITS OSTENTATIOUSNESS IS SO EXTREME THAT MANY PEOPLE ARE OVERCOME WITH FITS OF THE GIGGLES.

WHAT DO YOU... OH, MY GOD!

HEE... HEE... HA, HA! HA, HA, HA, HA!

OKAY? UNDER CONTROL?

YEAH... HEE, HEE, WAIT A MINUTE... HA, HA, HA!

MR. PRESIDENT!

YES, ROLAND.

SIR, AS YOU KNOW, THERE'S BEEN A LOT OF TALK RECENTLY ABOUT A SECRET SOCIETY YOU BELONG TO AT YALE.

IT'S SAID THAT THE GROUP WAS BEHIND THE RECENT THEFT OF MARTIN VAN BUREN'S SKULL. IT'S SAID THAT ITS MEMBERS HAVE GUARANTEED LIFETIME INCOMES. THERE'RE RUMORS OF RITUALISTIC NUDE WRESTLING.

OF COURSE, NONE OF THESE STORIES IS VERIFIABLE BECAUSE NO MEMBER HAS EVER BROKEN THE SOCIETY'S CODE OF ABSOLUTE SECRECY.

IN FACT, THE CODE IS SAID TO BE SO STRICT THAT MEMBERS ARE REQUIRED TO LEAVE THE ROOM IF ANY OUTSIDER SO MUCH AS **MEN-TIONS** THE GROUP'S NAME, SKULL AND BONES!

SIR, WOULD YOU CARE TO PUT TO REST THESE...

EXCUSE ME.

PARDON ME, COMING THROUGH!

HOLD MY CALLS, WILL YOU, DEAR? I WANT TO GO OVER THESE DEFICIT FIGURES BEFORE THE TOWN MEETING.

YOU GOT IT, CONGRESS-WOMAN.

I DON'T KNOW WHY SHE'S BOTHERING. THE ONLY THING PEOPLE WANT TO TALK ABOUT NOW IS AIDS.

HOW BAD IS IT HERE NOW, BRIAN?

WELL, WE STILL DON'T KNOW FOR SURE, BUT IT'S POSSIBLE THAT UP TO 70% OF SAN FRANCISCO GAYS ARE INFECTED. THOUSANDS ARE DYING RIGHT NOW...

I WON'T BE ASKED ABOUT BASEBALL, WILL I, DEAR? I DON'T KNOW ANYTHING ABOUT THE "A's".

I'LL FIELD THOSE, LACEY.

BRIAN, I DON'T SEE BILL GOETZ OR RANDY SIMS ON THE TOWN MEETING GUEST LIST...

I'M AFRAID THEY'RE BOTH IN THE HOSPITAL, BOSS.

IN THE HOSPITAL? OH, DEAR, HOW DREADFUL...

IT GETS WORSE. REMEMBER TAD BAILEY? FROM THE CAMPAIGN? HE DIED LAST WEEK.

WE'RE NOT TALKING ABOUT TRAFFIC ACCIDENTS HERE, ARE WE?

WELCOME HOME, BOSS.

AND BOTH BILL AND RANDY ARE IN THE HOSPITAL WITH IT, TOO?

YES, MA'AM. BILL ONLY HAS AIDS-RELATED COMPLEX, BUT RANDY HAS FULL-BLOWN KAPOSI'S SARCOMA.

I THINK YOU'LL FIND THAT AIDS WILL BE THE ONLY TOPIC AT YOUR TOWN MEETING TODAY. PEOPLE WILL WANT YOUR VIEWS ON **EVERYTHING**, FROM HEALTH CARE COSTS TO CONFIDENTIALITY ISSUES TO RE-LICENSING THE BATH HOUSES!

RE-LICENSING THE BATH HOUSES? YOU MEAN, THEY'RE **CLOSED?**

UH... YES, MA'AM. THEY HAVE BEEN FOR SOME TIME.

BUT I THOUGHT GOOD HYGIENE WAS EXACTLY THE ISSUE!

I BETTER GET THE BRIEFING BOOKS...

BRIAN, WHAT HOSPITAL ARE THOSE DEAR BOYS AT? I WANT TO SEND FLOWERS...

THEY'RE AT GENERAL. THERE'RE A FEW OTHER FORMER STAFFERS THERE AS WELL... ED HOBBS, ANDY LIPPINCOTT...

ANDY LIPPINCOTT? ANDY HAS... AIDS?

YES. FULL-BLOWN, AS THEY SAY IN THE AIDS BIZ.

OH, MY GOD...

YOU KNOW HIM? OH, HEY, I'M SORRY...

WE'RE QUITE THE ANGEL OF DEATH TODAY, AREN'T WE, DEAR?

HEY, C'MON, BOSS, SOMEONE HAS TO BRING YOU UP TO SPEED.

©B Trudeau

GOD, NO... NOT ANDY, TOO!

I'M SORRY TO BE THE ONE TO TELL YOU, JOANIE.

HOW BAD IS HE?

HE'S VERY SICK. HE'S GOT BOTH PNEUMONIA AND KS. BUT HE'S A FIGHTER. HIS MORALE IS HIGH.

HE'S ALSO GOT THE BEST DOCTOR IN THE CITY LOOKING AFTER HIM. THIS GUY KNOWS HOW TO CARE FOR AIDS PATIENTS.

YOU KNOW YOUR JAMMIES CLASH WITH YOUR LESIONS, DON'T YOU?

SO WHO ARE YOU, RALPH LAUREN?

©B Trudeau

HOW'S HE DOING?

WELL, HIS SPIRITS ARE GOOD, BUT YOU MIGHT BE A LITTLE SHOCKED BY HIS APPEARANCE. HE'S PRETTY EMACIATED.

OKAY. THANKS FOR THE WARNING...

VISITOR, MR. LIPPINCOTT!

JOANIE!

GASP!...

MISS? MISS?

YOU STILL MAKE 'EM SWOON, KID!

WELL, WOMEN, SURE. A LOT OF GOOD THAT DOES ME!

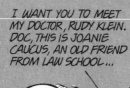

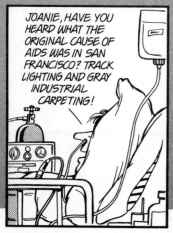

JOANIE, WHAT YOU HAVE TO UNDERSTAND IS THERE'S A LOT OF ANGER ON THIS WARD. FOR MOST PATIENTS, AIDS IS A STIGMA ON TOP OF A STIGMA. SOCIETY HAS YET TO COME TO TERMS WITH IT.

ANDY USES HUMOR TO SOFTEN THE RAGE HE FEELS AND TO HELP HIM FACE THE ABYSS. I ENCOURAGE IT, BECAUSE AIDS CARE IS ABOUT HELPING PEOPLE COPE, HELPING THEM DIE WITH DIGNITY...

EVERY DAY I GO IN TO SEE ANDY, AND HE MAKES SOME TERRIBLE JOKE ABOUT HIS LESIONS, AND I PLAY STRAIGHT MAN, AND WE'RE BOTH SCREAMING INSIDE, BUT IT'S BETTER THAN GOING MAD.

AND ON YOUR DAYS OFF?

I UNWIND. HOLD UP CONVENIENCE STORES. THAT SORT OF THING.

©B Trudeau

I'M AFRAID I CAN'T REALLY GIVE YOU A PROGNOSIS, JOANIE. ANDY'S SUFFERING FROM A HOST OF INFECTIONS, AND IT'S HARD TO PREDICT WHEN AND WHAT HE WILL ULTIMATELY DIE OF.

YOU CAN'T BELIEVE HOW LITTLE WE REALLY KNOW ABOUT AIDS. WE STILL DON'T EVEN KNOW HOW LONG THE LATENCY PERIOD IS. IT COULD BE AS MUCH AS 15 YEARS!

BACK-DATING?

UM... DOESN'T EVERYONE?

©B Trudeau

65

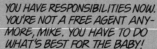

70

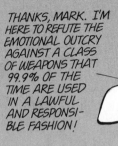

OKAY! WE GOT A MAJOR MAYBE FROM DISNEY! THEY'RE GONNA GET BACK TO ME!

I THINK WHAT WE GOTTA DO NOW IS SWEETEN THE POT, BRING IN ANOTHER BANKABLE ELEMENT! LIKE THE ACTRESS WE WANT TO PLAY OPPOSITE YOU!

ANY SUGGESTIONS?

YEAH, I GOT SOMEONE IN MIND. VERY CLASSY, BUT ACCESSIBLE. KIND OF A DRINKING MAN'S STREEP. BUT I'LL HAVE TO CHECK ON HER AVAILABILITY. SHE'S GOT A LOT OF HEAT ON HER NOW!

GREAT SCRIPT! WHAT HAPPENS TO YOUR ARM?

I DUNNO. I GUESS IT DECOMPOSES.

MR. PRESIDENT, I'LL LET YOU KNOW JUST AS SOON AS I HEAR SOMETHING!...HOLD ON, RON, THAT'S MY OTHER LINE! BE RIGHT BACK!

BURRR!

HELLO? YEAH...OKAY...GOOD! THANKS! GOODBYE...HELLO, RON? THAT WAS MY OFFICE. THEY'RE SENDING ME SOMETHING OVER THE CAR FAX! BET YOU A DINNER IT'S AN OFFER FROM DISNEY!

OKAY, YOU'RE ON!

HERE IT COMES...

WHIRRR

WELL?

IT'S A FAX OF SOMEONE SITTING ON MY XEROX MACHINE. WHERE DO YOU WANT TO EAT?

BAD BREAK, MR. PRESIDENT— DISNEY PASSED. BUT I'VE GOT CALLS IN TO THE STUDIO HEADS OF ALL THE OTHER MAJORS. AND A LOT OF THESE GUYS OWE ME!

THESE THINGS TAKE TIME, OKAY? SO DON'T GET DOWN! OKAY? RONNIE? HEY, KID, WHO LOVES YA? WILL YOU TELL ME THAT, BABE? WHO LOVES YOU?

WHAT?

UH...NO, SIR, I'M NOT MAKING A PASS AT YOU.

MR. SPIELBERG RETURNING YOUR CALL FROM LAST YEAR.

RICK, ASIDE FROM THE HONDURAS THING, HOW DO YOU THINK I'M DOING?

HON-ESTLY, SIR?

SURE! I LOVE THE GIVE-AND-TAKE WITH YOU BOYS IN THE PRESS!

WELL, SIR, I THINK THE WHITE HOUSE HAS BECOME REAC-TIVE, THAT IT'S BEING LED BY EVENTS.

EVERYONE'S WONDERING WHEN YOU'RE GOING TO STOP BEING EXCITED AND START BEING EXCITING. PEOPLE ARE WAITING FOR YOU TO BECOME MORE...WELL... LEADERLIKE!

RICK, WE'RE STUDYING THE LEADERSHIP THING. WE'RE TAKING A NO-HOLDS-BARRED LOOK AT IT!

SIR, COULD YOU HEAT THIS SUCKER UP, FOR ME, PLEASE?

...AND THIS IS THE MASTER BEDROOM! FEEL FREE TO POKE AROUND THE DRAWERS IF YOU LIKE!

IF YOU TURN ON THE CLOCK-RADIO, YOU'LL FIND IT'S TUNED TO COUNTRY MUSIC, JUST LIKE I PROMISED DURING THE CAMPAIGN!

AND THIS IS OUR PRIVATE BATHROOM! THIS IS WHERE I SHAVE! AND THIS IS WHERE I PUT MY PANTS ON!

WOULD THAT BE ONE LEG AT A TIME, SIR?

NO, I'M STILL TOO EXCITED! I JUMP INTO 'EM!

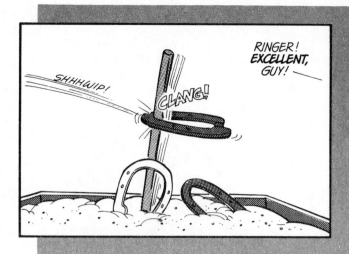

83

84

AN UNLIKELY MENTION IN THE WARHOL DIARIES.

I'M IN HIS DIARIES? BUT I NEVER *MET* THE MAN!

CHECK OUT PAGE 355, BOSS.

"APRIL 24, 1984, KEITH HARING THREW ONE OF HIS TANTRUMS BECAUSE NOBODY WAS TAKING HIS PICTURE, SO HE STORMED OFF THE PLANE AT MILAN, LEAVING JUST ME, WARREN AND JACK."

"WARREN HAD JUST RETURNED FROM WASHINGTON, WHERE HE WAS WRAPPING UP THREE OR FOUR AFFAIRS, INCLUDING ONE WITH CONGRESS-WOMAN LACEY DAVENPORT."

GRACIOUS! *THAT* SHOULD PEP UP MY IMAGE!

OH. HOLD OFF ON THE LAWSUIT, THEN?

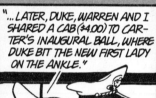

"...LATER, DUKE, WARREN AND I SHARED A CAB ($4.00) TO CARTER'S INAUGURAL BALL, WHERE DUKE BIT THE NEW FIRST LADY ON THE ANKLE."

WOW...DID YOU REALLY DO ALL THOSE THINGS, SIR?

IT'S POSSIBLE. I DON'T REMEMBER ANYTHING BETWEEN 1968 AND 1981.

NOTHING?

NADA. TOTAL BLANK.

AREN'T YOU A LITTLE CURIOUS?

ONLY ABOUT THE SCARS. IT LOOKS LIKE I HAD A BOTCHED APPENDECTOMY.

OKAY, LET'S *READ ON!* THIS LOOKS INTERESTING— IT'S ABOUT THE D.J.'S AT STUDIO 54... "LAST NIGHT THERE WAS A NEW D.J. WHO COULD REALLY DANCE AND DO A GOOD PATTER..."

"LIZA AND C.Z. AND JERRY THOUGHT HE WAS TALENTED, BUT FORGET IT. IN A FEW YEARS, HE'LL BE SOME NOBODY DOING A BORING TALK RADIO SHOW AT THREE IN THE MORNING."

*WHEW!* BRUTAL! THIS GUY REALLY TELLS IT LIKE IT... LIKE IT...

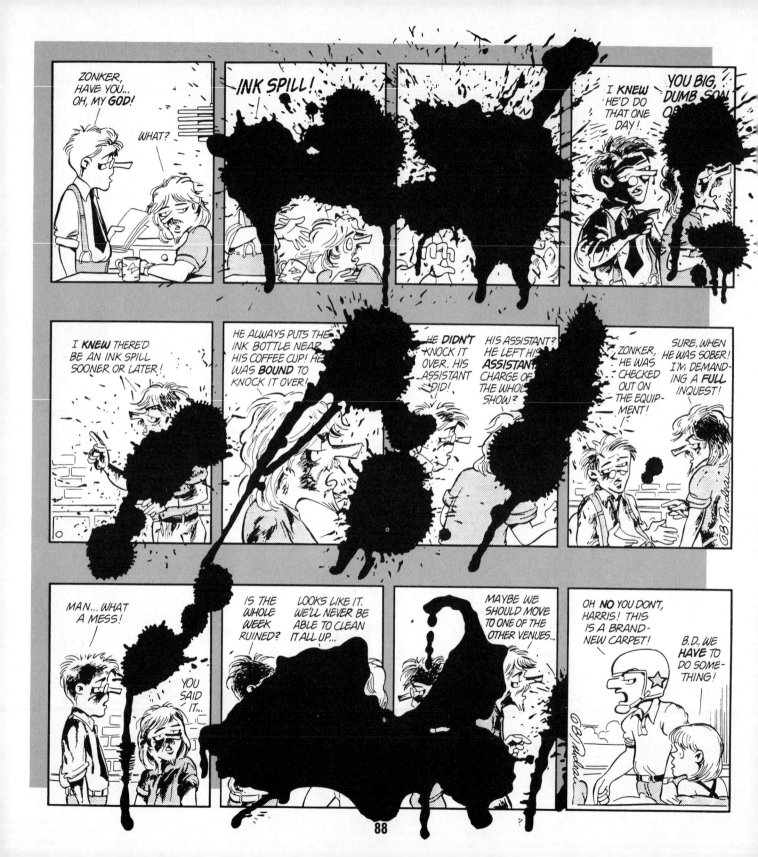

90

WE'D LIKE SMOKING, PLEASE.

YES, SIR. MAY I HAVE YOUR CREDIT CARD, PLEASE?

TAP! TAP! TAP!

THAT'S TWO FIRST-CLASS TICKETS TO LOS ANGELES, FULL FARE FOR YOU, AND HALF FARE FOR YOUR GRANDDAUGHTER.

MY GRAND-DAUGHTER?

HEY... IT'S YOU!

SHE'S MY FIANCEE!

OF COURSE SHE IS! WHAT AN HONOR, MR. HEFNER!

...AND FOR MORE ON THE HEFNER NUPTIALS, LET'S GO LIVE TO OUR ACTION NEWS HELI-COPTER NOW HOVER-ING OVER THE PLAYBOY MANSION!

MAN, HEF'S WEDDING IS ALL OVER THE NEWS!

I KNOW!

I'M SO EXCITED ABOUT BEING A BRIDES-MAID! LOOK WHAT KIMBERLEY SENT OVER TODAY!

YOU CARRY THAT?

NO, NO, I WEAR IT. LOOKS LIKE I'LL HAVE TO TAKE IT IN, THOUGH.

HERE COMES THE BRIDE... DA, DA, DA, DUM!

DOESN'T SHE LOOK DARLING IN HER WED-DING EN-SEMBLE, B.D.?

UH... WHO?

KIMBERLEY! ISN'T HER PRE-NUPTIAL CENTER-FOLD THE MOST FABU-LOUS THING YOU'VE EVER SEEN!

UH... WELL, I DUNNO, BOOPSIE. I MEAN, I ONLY BUY SKIN MAGS ONCE IN A WHILE, YOU KNOW, WHEN THERE'S AN ARTICLE I'M INTERESTED IN...

...BUT I'D SAY SHE'S RIGHT UP THERE WITH MISS MAY '83, MISS AUGUST '74 AND MISS JUNE '69.

YES, SHE'S VERY SPECIAL.

96